ABORTION

YES or NO?

By JOHN L. GRADY, M.D.
Foreword by SENATOR JESSE HELMS

8th Edition

Originally published by John L. Grady, M.D. in 1967.
Copyright © 1979 by John L. Grady, M.D.
Library of Congress Catalog Card Number: 79-53228.
ISBN: 0-089555-117-9.
Printed and bound in the United States of America.

> *"The hottest places in Hell*
> *are reserved for those who,*
> *in a period of moral crisis,*
> *maintain their neutrality."*
> *Dante*

TAN BOOKS AND PUBLISHERS, INC.
Rockford, Illinois 61105

United States Senate

The issue of abortion has not only caused a great deal of controversy, it has been subject to profound misinformation. For example, the slogan that abortion is a woman's right to control her own body sounds fine . . . every person should have the right to be free from unjustified invasions of his or her physical integrity—but since when does a pregnant woman's "own body" have two different heart beats, two different sets of brain waves, and two different blood types? Dr. John Grady has used his years of experience as a physician to consider this question and many of the complex medical and ethical problems surrounding the present abortion controversy.

Abortion—Yes or No has been widely acclaimed by physicians, judges, clergy, educators, social workers, adults and teenagers, and it has been of immeasurable value to those individuals honestly seeking a factual and logical understanding of the subject—especially young women who may be weighing a personal decision regarding abortion.

One of the first booklets written on the subject of abortion, it has been regularly revised and updated through seven editions, from the first text written in 1966 to this present edition published in 1979. It is probably one of the most widely read and heard dissertations on abortion in the world.

Dr. Grady presents his material in a clear and reasonable manner so that any intelligent person, without professional or technical training, can quickly comprehend the facts and make a reasonable judgement.

The practice of abortion is one of the foremost moral issues confronting the American people today. I challenge you to take the few minutes necessary to read this short treatise.

SENATOR JESSE HELMS

ABORTION: YES OR NO

INTRODUCTION

Because abortion, right or wrong, is a very serious matter, an objective, unemotional analysis of the subject is in order. This treatise contains definite opinions, to be sure, but supported by reason and fact, hopefully to your satisfaction. There are no misquotes, altered data, or intentional misrepresentations of any kind. The conclusions and summaries herein are supported by logical arguments and reliable opinions from respected authorities in various fields. Where the statement is relative to medicine or science, the educational or technical background of the authority is noted. Where the statement pertains to philosophy or theology, the personal or religious background of the authority is noted.

Equal coverage to all aspects of the subject or to all views is not intended or implied. I do not represent this treatise as being a complete text or its author as being infallible. I ask you to be as honest and objective as you read it.

Bear in mind that laws against abortion and traditional concepts regarding the termination of fetal life have existed for hundreds of years. This, together with the magnitude of the issue, places the burden of proof for change upon those demanding it.

RECENT HISTORY

In the years prior to 1965, abortion was rarely discussed, either in public or in private. Abortion was generally considered to be "bad" or "evil," and even those who in any way approved of or tolerated abortion recognized the discussion of the subject to be in poor taste. However, with the rapid evolution of our present "permissive age," a few organizations and individuals became vocal on the subject and were given considerable exposure in the news media. The American press and television, being essentially and predominantly liberal, began saturation reporting of the subject as "abortion reform," and rapidly became pro-abortion in both reporting and editorial policy. Thus, another "critical issue" was created by slanted reporting in the mass communications media.

Abortion became a headline word in newspapers and the subject of feature articles in magazines and journals. It provoked discussion in the home, argument and division in medical and legal societies, and bitter debate in state legislatures. Opponents have held the centuries-old view that it is immoral, an ugly, shameful act, and a crime. Proponents speak of it as desirable, an act of mercy and compassion, and want it legalized.

Unfortunately, most magazine and newspaper articles have been sensational, emotional, and not very factual. Likewise, most television reports and documentaries have been incomplete, and have presented only one side of the issue. Consequently, the public opinion which has been formed often has been based on misrepresentations and limited information. Data and statistics presented by both sides have been badly exaggerated and misused.

Regardless of one's sincerity, motivation and present opinion, he should recognize that the issue of abortion was intentionally created, and that the mass media push and the legislative push were both planned and coordinated. Please be assured that there is ample evidence of this fact in written articles, editorials, and publications printed specifically for legislative bodies. It can be stated surely and factually that there was never a grassroots movement or ground swell of public opinion to legalize abortion. Undeniable is the fact that, prior to 1966, the general pattern of the law in all 50 states was prohibition of abortion, except to preserve the life of the mother. These laws were clearly understood by physicians, lawyers, pregnant women, and the general public. In many states the laws had been in existence for a century or more and were well accepted.

But in 1967, liberal abortion legislation was introduced in 35 states in almost identical form, primarily through the efforts of three organizations—the American Law Institute, Planned Parenthood-World Population, and the American Civil Liberties Union (A.C.L.U.).

STATUS OF THE LAW

There continues to be so much legislative and court activity regarding abortion that any summary of the law may be inaccurate by the time it is published. Nevertheless, let us summarize in brief. From 1966 through 1970, 16 states revised their abortion laws, varying from very minor modification (Mississippi) to near abortion on demand (New York). During this same period hundreds of liberal abortion bills were defeated throughout the United States.

Initially, pro-abortion forces were moderately successful, but by 1971, pro-life organizations were functioning well. No major abortion legislation passed in any state in 1971, and liberal abortion bills were defeated in at least 28 states. Some states which had enacted the new abortion laws began to reverse their liberal position. For example, in New York the experience with permissive abortion became so repugnant that in May, 1972, the State Legislature passed a bill repealing the two-year-old liberal abortion law and reinstating the old statute permitting abortions only to save the life of the mother. Nelson Rockefeller, then governor of the state, vetoed the bill.

However, when the pro-abortion movement was slowed to a stop in the state legislatures, the battle shifted to the courts. Soon there were many conflicting decisions and reversals of decisions by state supreme courts and federal courts. Several state supreme courts upheld the constitutionality of their long-established and restrictive state abortion laws, while a few suddenly found them unconstitutionally vague or restrictive. In Florida (1972) the State Supreme Court, in effect, outlined new liberal legislation and set down a specific time limit in which an acceptable abortion bill was to be passed by the legislature. Regardless of one's attitude towards abortion, he would have to recognize this as one of the most audacious usurpations of legislative authority by a state court in the history of the American judicial system.

It was inevitable that the matter would ultimately be heard by the United States Supreme Court. In its first approach to the subject, the Supreme Court's action tended to uphold the constitutionality of existing state laws and indicated the necessity of protective laws for the unborn baby. However, this decision concerned a specific and limited application of the law, and the court agreed to review the entire matter in depth. Finally, on Monday, January 22, 1973, in a seven-to-two decision, the Supreme Court struck down all restrictive laws against abortion and, in effect, prohibited the states from having any compelling interest in the protection of the fetus until it is "viable" or "capable of meaningful life." This meant abortion on demand throughout the first six or seven months of pregnancy. Furthermore, after that time, the state could not prevent an abortion undertaken to preserve the "health" of the mother, which by the U.N. World Health Organization's definition means complete social well being—physical, emotional, psychological, familial, age, and general well being. Clearly, then, the Supreme Court mandated abortion on demand.

While the pro-abortion forces claim total and final victory, most pro-life organizations are working towards the passage of a constitutional amendment, protecting the right to life of all citizens from the moment of conception until natural death. While many of those who oppose the Supreme Court's decision take up the monumental and formidable task of a constitutional amendment, others believe that Congress itself can solve the problem. The eminent Dean Clarence Manion, a respected constitutional authority, has pointed out that Congress has the power "to regulate, restrict or entirely abrogate the jurisdiction of the inferior Federal Courts" as well as the power of "control over the appellate jurisdiction of the Supreme Court." Thus, if Congress removed the jurisdiction of the Federal Courts over any particular issue (such as abortion, education, busing, prayer in school, etc.), the determination of that issue would then return to the respective states.

Still other authorities on constitutional law, such as T. David Horton, of Nevada, declare that the Supreme Court's decision itself was unconstitutional, insofar as only state legislatures have the constitutional authority to make and unmake state law. Therefore, the U.S. Supreme Court's action was an *ultra vires* act (i.e., illegal), because it exceeds the constitutional authority of that governmental body to so act. Therefore, state laws restricting abortion remain in effect. This same opinion has also been stated by several state attorneys general.

Whatever the status of the law now, and no matter how it is interpreted and accepted by opposing forces, one thing is clear— the battle has just begun.

DEFINITIONS

Webster's dictionary defines *abortion* as the expulsion of the human fetus prematurely. A medical dictionary defines it similarly, but lists some twenty-two classifications or types of abortions; for example, accidental, criminal, habitual, induced, infectious, natural, and therapeutic. Obviously, the legislation in question does not deal with the usual accidental or natural cause of an abortion or "miscarriage," such as intrauterine infection, incompetent cervix, trauma, and the like. Rather, the question now before the people and their legislators is whether or not there should be restrictions on what Webster calls *aborticide;* that is, the act of destroying a fetus in the womb, either by direct use of instruments or by the use of a chemical or "medication" that kills the fetus and/or causes it to be expelled.

ABORTION ARGUMENTS CLASSIFIED

Most of the arguments in favor of abortion fall into one or more of the following medical, social, or economic categories or situations which demonstrate the hardships and dangers of pregnancy, and conclude that liberalization of traditional laws against abortion will permit solution of these problems:

1. The baby is a threat to the mother's physical or mental well-being.
2. The baby is the result of rape or incest. Also included in this category, in the more liberal proposals, is the "unwanted baby"—unwanted because it is illegitimate, or because the mother is "too young" (the proposed age under which any girl may automatically qualify for an abortion usually being 16 years). Additional reasons given are that either or both parents are of low intelligence or poor character, or that the baby will be an economic "burden" to the family or the state.
3. There is a possibility the baby will be physically deformed, mentally retarded, or in some other way imperfect. The cases cited usually assume that the fetus was exposed to some physically damaging drug, chemical, or disease (such as Thalidomide, LSD or German measles). These are frequently referred to as the "fetal indications" for abortion.
4. The mother alone should have the authority or right to determine if a pregnancy is to be carried to term, and how many, if any, living children she is to bear; that abortion is a personal matter between a woman and her doctor; and that she has the right to rid herself of any unwanted pregnancy. Furthermore, it is argued that abortion is a backup for contraceptive failure and, as such, is also an acceptable means of population control.
5. Abortions have always been performed throughout the United States. Some were being done in hospitals by doctors, in violation of the law. However, in the past, the majority of abortions were performed by non-medical personnel outside the hospital—criminal abortions. Furthermore, the woman or girl who had a criminal abortion was subjected to possible injury and even death, because of infection or other physical damage from improper or unsterile technique, since the physician was not able to perform the abortion in a hospital. It

is stated that legalized abortion will eliminate the criminal abortionist. It is further argued that since abortion is legal in some other countries, it should be permitted in the United States.

PERFORMING AN ABORTION

Methods used or attempted by criminal abortionists are varied and frequently inept, although usually the techniques are similar to the legal abortionists' (i.e., those used by doctors and para-medical personnel). In addition, there have been recent articles or instructions on the techniques of "do it yourself" abortion. We have neither the space nor the wish to elaborate on any of these pathetic and ignorant acts.

A method of abortion recently developed is the use of a hormone chemical (prostaglandin) which, when taken either orally or by injection, causes the sloughing off of the lining of the uterus, even without pregnancy. In early pregnancy, it stimulates spontaneous emptying of the uterus. Hence, the name M-Pill (for menstruation) or A-Pill (for abortion). This drug is just coming into widespread use in the United States, and advocates of abortion are enthusiastic over its potential. With general and regular use, it could eliminate the necessity of contraception, could be taken monthly to cause a regular menstrual period, and would allegedly alleviate a woman's anxiety and guilt about committing an abortion—because she never knows if she is pregnant or not.

Usually, the human embryo is at least four to six weeks old when pregnancy is first confirmed. Abortion techniques currently used depend primarily on the stage of pregnancy, as follows:

1. Up to twelve weeks, the usual method of abortion is the suction technique, the dilatation and curettage (D and C) technique, or a combination of the two. In the suction procedure, the cervix (mouth of the uterus) is dilated (stretched) by inserting progressively larger instruments until it is open enough to insert a tube which is attached to a strong suction apparatus. The embryo, or small fetus, is sucked out into a collecting bottle, is crushed or badly torn while being sucked out, and immediately dies from the trauma and the loss of blood supply and oxygen. Curettage (scraping out to clean the uterus) is usually done with or following the suction technique, to insure a complete job.
2. When the dilatation and curettage method is used alone,

following the dilatation of the cervix, a sharp, loop-shaped instrument (curette) is inserted into the uterus, and the fetus, placenta and membranes are cut up and pulled out and the inner walls of the uterus scraped until clean. By the twelfth week, the fetus has eyes, ears, arms, legs, finger and toe nails, and all its organs. A fetus at this stage is capable of moving and feeling pain. After twelve weeks (see picture—The Human Fetus), the head and extremities are often too large to pull out intact and are cut up or crushed by forceps before being extracted.

3. The usual abortion method after 12-14 weeks is stimulation of premature labor. This can be done by the intravenous or intramuscular injection of oxytocic medications, but is most frequently done by injecting a foreign substance into the uterine cavity. A long needle is inserted through the abdomen and the uterine wall into the uterus. The normal amniotic fluid around the baby is withdrawn and replaced by glucose (sugar), saline (salt), or other chemical solutions. This "salting out procedure" usually kills the baby prior to, or during, the ensuing labor. However, the baby may be delivered alive, and frequently is large enough and strong enough to live if it were given maximum care.

4. The least used method is hysterotomy, done only in advanced pregnancy. The uterus is entered through an abdominal incision and the baby removed. Hysterotomy is identical to cesarean section, except that in the latter the baby is saved; in the former it is killed and discarded.

In instances of abortion when the baby is delivered alive, it is killed by one of several means: placing it in a plastic bag (suffocation), leaving it in a container on the surgical table or in the refrigerator (exposure), or putting it into a container of water or formaldehyde (drowning). It is subsequently burned in an incinerator. However, in some medical centers, fetuses aborted alive are now being used for live research specimens.

Abortion cases are on record in which the infants were born alive and were so large and strong that they survived the abortion and were taken to the hospital nursery. Later these babies were adopted out to loving parents.

ARGUMENTS AGAINST ABORTION

Those against liberalization of the abortion laws take the position that the fetus, or baby, is a living human being and as such has every right to life. They state this simply and

IT NEVER HAD A CHANCE

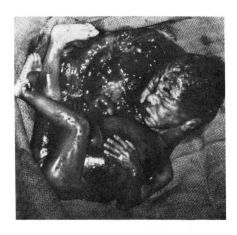

This 19-week-old baby was killed and aborted by the injection of saline into the uterus. (Picture reprinted with permission, Handbook on Abortion, *Wilke, Hiltz Publishing Company.)*

ALL IN A DAY'S WORK

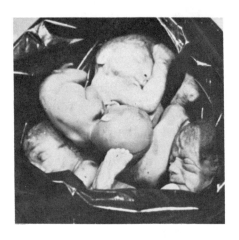

These babies were all aborted alive, by hysterotomy, in one morning at a large, metropolitan, university-affiliated hospital. (Picture reprinted with permission, Handbook on Abortion, *Wilke, Hiltz Publishing Company.)*

categorically, bringing multiple arguments to bear that show legally, morally, and medically that this has been the commonly accepted concept throughout the history of Western civilization.

They cite the United Nations Charter on Human Rights, written in 1948, which guarantees to every person the right to life; that children should be given special consideration in the law; and that the right to life should be guaranteed before as well as after birth. In addition, the opponents to abortion present the following counter-arguments against the aforementioned categories advanced by the proponents of abortion:

MEDICAL INDICATIONS

Opponents to abortion state that there are really few instances where the baby actually threatens the life of the mother. They easily support this assertion with the fact that many recognized medical authorities in the field of obstetrics and gynecology have clearly stated that, in the present day of excellent medical and surgical care, the situation rarely if ever exists where the baby must be sacrificed to preserve the life of the mother. Perhaps the most famous statement relative to abortion was made by Dr. Roy S. Heffernan, of Tufts University, to the Congress of The American College of Surgeons: "Anyone who performs a therapeutic abortion is either ignorant of modern methods of treating the complications of pregnancy or is unwilling to take the time to use them."

According to Dr. Joseph P. Donnelly, former Medical Director of Margaret Hague Hospital, New Jersey, "Abortion is never necessary to save the life of the mother." There were 115,000 deliveries at this maternity hospital from 1947 to 1961, during which time no abortions were done. Dr. Edwin DeCosta, Professor of Obstetrics and Gynecology, Northwestern University Medical School, (who favors abortion for social and economic reasons) states, "Strictly speaking and from the viewpoint of obstetrical and medical indications, there are few reasons today to perform therapeutic abortions." Dr. Leo T. Heywood, Professor of Obstetrics and Gynecology and Chairman of the Department at Creighton University School of Medicine in Omaha said, "I am against abortion. It is not necessary in the practice of medicine, and it destroys the very thing the physician is dedicated to preserve—human life." States Dr. Bernard J. Pisani, Professor of Obstetrics and Gynecology, New York University School of Medicine, "Medical reasons for provoking abortion are just about

11

non-existent. In fact, no basis on pure medical grounds ever really stands up."

In addition, thousands of physicians across the United States, each of whom has cared for hundreds of mothers and infants during their respective years of practice, state firmly they have never in these thousands of pregnancies seen a single instance where the infant had to be sacrificed to save the mother, nor have they seen a situation where a mother has been lost for failure of the physician to perform an abortion. In fact, in more than thirteen years of obstetrical practice, I never lost a mother from any cause. Moreover, during that time, at the public hospital where I was a staff member, there were thousands of babies delivered and, to my knowledge, not a single therapeutic abortion. Thus, with today's advanced medical knowledge and practice, a "therapeutic" abortion is never necessary, because competent physicians, using the latest medical and surgical techniques, can preserve the lives of both the mother and the child.

PSYCHIATRIC INDICATIONS

Since the Supreme Court's decision, permitting abortion essentially on demand, mental health indications account for as high as 97 percent of the total number of abortions performed.

Doctors opposed to abortion strongly state that no one has ever established a cause-and-effect relationship between pregnancy and mental illness. Women who are emotionally unstable get pregnant, but pregnancy is not the *cause* of their illness. These doctors consider the argument that a pregnancy might threaten the mental well-being of the mother as vague, based on a situation which is extremely rare, and certain to be subjected to much abuse by "nervous mothers" and "eager doctors." The opponents of abortion feel that "emotional stress" of the mother is not sufficient cause to warrant destruction of her baby.

John Phelan, M.D., Instructor of Psychiatry, University of Miami School of Medicine, states, "I share the opinion of many of my colleagues that there are no psychiatric indications for abortion. We hear that abortion is necessary to protect the mental health of the mother or that, unless an abortion is performed, a patient will commit suicide. This approach is fallacious and does not stand up under statistical and clinical scrutiny." Dr. Howard C. Taylor, Jr., Director of Obstetrics and Gynecology at Columbia-Presbyterian Medical Center, New

York, states, "I have not in my experience ever run across a suicide in pregnancy in a patient suffering from anxiety depression." Dr. Milton Halpern, Chief Medical Examiner of New York City, states that he can ". . . hardly recall an autopsy on a death by suicide during the last 25 years which revealed pregnancy." Also, the Coroner for the City of Birmingham investigated all female suicides for the period 1950 through 1956 and concluded, "We have no record of any women known to be pregnant having committed suicide." An accurate ten-year study was done in England on unwed mothers who requested abortions, and were refused. It was found that the suicide rate of this group was less than that of the average population.

Psychiatrist Robert J. Campbell, M.D., of New York City, points out that for many patients pregnancy and childbirth seem to exert a beneficial effect on their mental status. He further states that, "The grossly unstable seem to tolerate pregnancy remarkably well . . . better than they tolerate therapeutic abortion." Dr. Theodore Lidz, Professor of Psychiatry at Yale University School of Medicine, seems to agree: "It is practically impossible . . . to predict when an abortion will not be more detrimental to the mental health than the carrying of the child to birth."

Here is the opinion of Dr. Ben Sheppard of Miami, nationally known physician, attorney, Juvenile Court Judge, lecturer, writer, and Chairman of the National Council on Crime and Delinquency: "Young adolescents who have had abortions may verbalize relief to please adults, but this is never their internal feeling. Their psychic trauma and loss of personal morality will persist throughout life."

The vast majority of physicians who practice obstetrics have never had a pregnant woman become frankly psychotic or commit suicide. They point out that many of those who are fearful, disturbed, or perhaps have even threatened suicide early in the pregnancy, actually improve as the pregnancy progresses. This is particularly true of the unmarried. Dr. Walter Dillon, Professor of Obstetrics and Gynecology, Stritch School of Medicine, and Chairman of OB-GYN at South Shore Hospital, Chicago, relates that, "Pregnancy in the unwed causes nervous moments but to which the patient makes adequate adjustments. For a number of years I have been in charge of a clinic for unwed girls, and mental disturbances have not been a problem . . . I personally cannot justify a direct abortion for any reason . . . the fetus has a right to be born."

There are many cases where the mother has spoken of abortion early in pregnancy and, later on, has confessed her gratitude to the physician for not having performed the abortion. It is a fact that most women who have been unhappy to find they were pregnant have been most happy with the baby that resulted from that pregnancy. On the other hand, I have studied case histories of married women who have become troubled, consumed with guilt, and developed significant psychiatric problems following, and because of, abortion. I believe it can be stated with certainty that abortion causes more deep-seated guilt, depression, and mental illness than it ever cures.

RAPE—INCEST—ILLEGITIMACY

Opponents to abortion quickly agree that pregnancy resulting from rape or incest is a tragedy. Moreover, in these cases, as well as illegitimacy, there is an emotional as well as a social stigma involved. But is the psychic scar already inflicted on the mother not further compounded by the guilt of having destroyed that living being which was at least half her own? The reason to destroy a fetus may appear good, but can it in any way equal the wrong committed by the destruction of that infant? Do two wrongs make a right?

For centuries, traditional Jewish law has clearly stated that if a father sins against his daughter (incest), that does not justify a second wrong—the abortion of the product of that sin. This was reconfirmed by the New Jersey Orthodox Rabbinic Council in 1969, when it declared that, "Even if the fetus is the product of incest or rape, or an abnormality of any kind is foreseen, the right to life is still his."

The right of the baby to live certainly outweighs the license of a parent, a doctor, or any other individual to exterminate it. Even when there is a social crime perpetrated upon the girl, as in the case of rape, the unborn child is an innocent being in no way responsible for the offense, and should not be punished for the crime or misjudgement of either parent. Throughout history, pregnant women, sentenced to die for one crime or another, were given a stay of execution until after the delivery of the child. It was the contention of the courts that one could not punish the innocent child for the crime of the mother.

Although pregnancies can result from forcible rape, some women also have "cried rape" following voluntary intercourse, when they discovered they were pregnant. This should never be allowed as an excuse for abortion. However, everything should be done to prevent pregnancy from occurring in the victims of real rape. Additional research in this area should be implemented. *But we are talking here about preventing pregnancy, not terminating life.* When real rape has occurred, the victim should be promptly treated with vaginal irrigations and spermacides to prevent conception, and antibiotics should be given to prevent infection. However, pregnancy from rape is very uncommon. In humans, pregnancy occurs on the average of once in every 250-350 acts of intercourse. In rape, pregnancy occurs even less often, in fact, almost never, due to the stress factor. Thus, a highly emotional issue has been made of a statistically rare problem.

It's time we went to the cause of our problems. Let parents give their children wholesome sex education. And, at the same time, let us get tough on pornography and "adult" movies. Let us clean up our news-stands, our literature, and our television programs which encourage crime and abuse of drugs and which make a mockery of morality and good behavior and thereby contribute to rape and illegitimacy. I plead that we stop our permissiveness and direct our attention to preventing these problems and not towards abortion itself.

No one denies that it is unfortunate when pregnancy occurs in the single girl, the extremely young, or the mentally retarded. Pregnancy can also be a great hardship among the poor with large families, or in areas of so-called "population explosion." But because a pregnancy is not wanted, may we eradicate the fetus for our personal convenience? First, it should be demonstrated from history that many of our greatest individuals were born as the result of unexpected or unwanted pregnancies. Indeed, many of us living today were probably not planned or eagerly anticipated. Secondly, what of the rights of the unborn? Will we now reverse the precedents in our law which have held that an infant *in utero* is a person under the law, and does have rights— property rights, recourse for damages, and basic inherent constitutional rights? Let us recall those great American documents, The Declaration of Independence and the Constitution (14th Amendment), which clearly state that "all men are endowed by their Creator with certain inalienable rights . . . life, liberty and the pursuit of happiness," and that "no state shall make or enforce any law which shall . . . deprive any person of life, liberty, or property without due process of law." In abortion, who represents the unborn child? Where is his defense attorney?

Where is his due process of law, including the right to appeal his sentence of extermination?

FETAL INDICATIONS

Arguments for abortion elicit much emotion when the possibility of a deformed fetus is presented. There has been great attention given to this aspect of abortion because of the deformities which were caused by the drug Thalidomide several years ago, the current LSD menace, and the relatively large number of fetal deformities still resulting from German measles. It is acknowledged that, on occasion, some mother will consume drugs or chemicals, receive radiation, or contract some illness, such as rubella (German measles), that may damage the fetus she is carrying. However, because some percentage of these babies so exposed will have physical defects, is it reasonable that all those exposed should be subjected to aborticide? Perhaps one of the most pointed arguments was presented several years ago by a noted physician and medical educator who held degrees in the fields of public health and preventative medicine. This educator stated, "Of those women who have German measles during pregnancy, it is doubtful that more than one in ten will have babies with serious physical impairment. Now, I ask you, do we have the right to decide that the sickly should not have life? I do not think so. But, for the sake of argument, let us say that defective fetuses should be destroyed. Even then, does it follow that nine normal pregnancies should be aborted, along with the one abnormal? It would be ninety percent more humane to wait until all ten are born, then kill the affected one."

There is no evidence to indicate that an infant with congenital defects would rather not be born, since he cannot be consulted. This evidence might exist if suicides were common among people with congenital handicaps. However, to the contrary, these people seem to value life, for their incidence of suicide is less than that of the general population. Consider the New Jersey Supreme Court decision of 1967, which states in part, "If (the unborn child) could have been asked as to whether his life should be snuffed out before his full term of gestation could run its course, our felt intuition of human nature tells us he would almost surely choose life with defects as against no life at all . . . The right to life is inalienable in our society . . . The sanctity of the simple human life is the decisive factor in this suit . . ."

Andre E. Hellegers, M.D., of The Johns Hopkins Hospital, in his excellent paper on abortion, states that, "While it is easier to feel that abortion is being performed for the sake of the fetus, honesty requires us to recognize that we perform it for adults." And, Dr. Herbert Ratner, Director of Public Health at Oak Park, Illinois, states that, "Most doctors feel something unwholesome and unsavory about therapeutic abortion, because whatever it may do for the mother, they know it obviously can't be very therapeutic for the baby."

Abortion is a negative approach to "fetal problems." I suggest we take a positive approach. Expedite immunization against German measles. Crack down on drug abuse. Encourage doctors to give more responsible attention to distribution, availability and use of drugs. There are adequate, effective medications now available to care for the pregnant woman, without using new and untried drugs.

Finally, we must consider future and personal implications: If we now decide we can kill the unborn, because of physical impairment, then why not those already born? For, if a pregnancy and the resulting child can be aborted (because it will be a mental or economic stress to the mother or family, or the baby will be "imperfect") then what of those many cases where a child, now living, is blind or deaf or has sustained crippling injuries? Indeed, what of the aged, who have become a burden to society? What are we to do with them? Because they are no longer self-sufficient, like the infant in the womb, should they then be subjected to euthanasia? And if the doctor, the mother, and the legislator can combine in their judgment to decide that a baby is not to live, then who in turn is to decide when the mother, the doctor, or the legislator may not live?

MOTHER'S RIGHT TO ABORTION

There are those who contend that the mother, alone, should have the right to determine how many babies she will have. This argument is erroneous insofar as it completely excludes the husband from having any interest or privilege in establishing the family. (And we certainly hold the traditional view that children should be conceived in marriage and raised in the home.) However, this argument is completely irrelevant because it substitutes "birth control" for abortion and confuses the issues. We are not discussing in this treatise the issue of birth control or contraception, which concerns how many babies any woman shall conceive. The issue is how many shall be permitted to live once conceived? Every reader must surely recognize that there is a lifetime worth of difference between "family planning" and "baby riddance." As the Protestant Theologian, Professor Helmut Thielicke of the University of Hamburg, stated, "Once impregnation has taken place, it is no longer a question of whether the parents concerned have the responsibility for a possible parenthood; they have already become parents." If a man and woman engage in sexual intercourse when a possible pregnancy will occur, then they must likewise accept the responsibility for any pregnancy which may result.

The argument that "a woman has the right to control her own body" may be correct, but it is not the issue at this point. Because, once she is pregnant, that fetus is entirely separate, distinct, and unique. It is not part of her body, but only dependent on her body for nutrition and a safe environment. We hear a great deal about the rights and wishes of the mother and society in general, but little about the rights of the unborn. Dr. Eugene Diamond, Professor of Clinical Pediatrics, Loyola University, speaks thus for the fetus: "I speak for him intact or deformed, wanted or unwanted, illegitimate or high-born. I am for life and the preservation of life. I believe that any life is of infinite value and that this value is not significantly diminished by the circumstances of that life's beginning. I believe that this regard for life is the cornerstone of Western culture. I believe our patients are best served by medical ethics which hold this principle sacred."

Reverend Charles Carroll, Episcopal Priest and Chaplain to the University of California, San Francisco Medical Center, in his brilliant letter on abortion states, "I believe that the ultimate purpose of the state is to protect the innocent and those who cannot protect themselves. Have we not the vision, compassion, and means to care for the mother, save the child, place him in a childless home if need be, and afford him the right to life? A right not validly subject to majority vote! Catholics are not alone opposed to "liberalized" abortion, but also many Christians and Jews who respect the common law heritage of Anglo-American jurisprudence. How many innocents would we, through abortion legislation, sentence to death? Let us not do inadvertently what the Nazis did with deliberate intent."

When the German physicians subordinated their ethics to the plan of Hitler, they became, as Dr. Andrew C. Ivy stated at Nuremburg, ". . . servants of the state, healers on the one hand, respected murderers on the other." It was this loss of principle by the medical profession which subsequently prompted the Geneva Declaration of the World Health Organization, which states, "I will maintain the utmost respect for human life from the time of conception; even under threat I will not use my medical knowledge contrary to the laws of humanity."

Dr. E. J. Daniels, Baptist minister and nationally respected evangelist, stated publicly, "I want it understood that I stand with Dr. Grady in his position. Abortion is not less than murder. Furthermore, people deep down realize this, for I have had women who were grandmothers come to me emotional wrecks because of the haunting memories of abortions committed earlier in life." Dr. George Huntston Williams, Professor of Divinity at Harvard University, states that *next to achieving peace in the world, the second major moral issue of our society must be resolute opposition to abortion and euthanasia.*

Rabbi Meyer Cohen, Executive Director of The Union of Orthodox Rabbis of the U.S. and Canada, recently stated that abortion is a transgression against religion and humanity, a violation of Jewish law, and doubly sinful and repugnant because the unborn child is innocent and defenseless. Dr. Percy Collette, missionary with the non-denominational Boa Vista Foreign Missions, writes, "Abortion has been done by some Indian tribes in South America for hundreds of years. Those tribes which have practiced abortion have become almost extinct, deteriorating into small sadistic groups, mostly males, losing the ability to reproduce; while those who have a high code of ethics have survived, multiplied and are healthier. Life begins at conception, and to destroy this God-given gift to man is to destroy the whole human plan. To take the life of an unborn child, regardless of the number of days it has been forming, is murder."

CRIMINAL ABORTION

One of the commonly heard arguments for abortion is that, by not permitting abortions in our hospitals, we "force" thousands of abortions to be done in the back rooms by untrained personnel; and that, humanely, we would be doing women justice to afford them the protection of abortion by competent medical personnel, for the reasons previously mentioned. The opponents to abortion do not deny that criminal abortions are performed in great numbers, now as they always have been, and that certainly an abortion by a physician in a licensed hospital accomplishes the end desired in a rapid and generally safe manner. However, no abortion, especially after the first few weeks of pregnancy, is ever an innocuous procedure, completely free from danger and complications, as evidenced by Dr. Ratner's data: "In 1963 for the whole United States there were 275 deaths attributed to abortion of any kind. Of these, 114 were due to abortions that were criminal, self-induced or without legal indications, and 161 were due to legal abortions." In other words, more women died as the result of "safe" legal abortions than from illegal ones.

Moreoever, it can hardly be said that, because it is being done, we should make it legal. The same type of thinking can be applied to theft, murder, or any other crime. The fact that some people, or even that many people, are going to do it if they can, does not mean that it is right, nor that it should be made easy for them. True, we cannot legislate morality; but, to the contrary, our legislatures and courts can, and sometimes do, legalize activities and procedures that facilitate immorality.

It can be shown, statistically, that in countries and states where abortion has been legalized, the number of legal abortions has far exceeded that number which those favoring abortion said would be performed for "truly valid" reasons. In addition to this, there has been an astronomical increase in criminal abortion, both by doctors and by incompetent personnel outside hospitals.

To quote the editor of the *Obstetrical and Gynecological Survey,* "Now much as it goes against the grain to say so, there are quite a few gullible fellows in the medical profession—especially when a few dollars are involved . . ." And, again let me quote the great Dr. Ratner: "Let us not forget that the liberty to abort makes the physician more like a god than is good for him. Abortions are also lucrative. We know that, in the effort to please patients, some of the profession have a talent for descending to the lowest common denominator. If, today, some licensed physicians practicing in approved hospitals disregard both the letter and the spirit of the law by performing abortions that are in no way necessary for the preservation of the mother's life, what reason is there to believe that tomorrow, were the law made more liberal, physicians would be more respectful of it? We will then hear the old refrain by a larger chorus, 'If I don't do it, somebody else will.' "

Every physician will admit that, no matter how thoroughly policed any medical society or hospital staff may be, there are always a few doctors who are unethical, or who do medical and surgical procedures which are questionably necessary or ethical. When the rules are relaxed, these individuals capitalize on it, usually for monetary reasons. A sad example is the commercial profit-making which occurred in New York in the first two years of a liberal abortion law. "Abortion specialists," "abortion clinics," and "abortion referral agencies" sprang up by the score; and physicians throughout the United States were flooded with advertisements from agencies and hospitals soliciting business. It has been estimated by state health authorities that 250,000 babies were aborted the first year. At $500.00 each, incuding travel fare, physicians fees, clinic or hospital charges and referral and advertising fees, that amounted to a $125 million "legal" (not including illegal) extermination business in New York in one year. Today, the business is much bigger and more widespread.

Doctors should never forget their great Oath of Hippocrates, the guiding principle for physicians for centuries, which states, "To none will I give a deadly drug, even if solicited, nor offer counsel to such an end, and to no woman will I give a destructive suppository, but guiltless and hallowed will I keep my art."

IS IT HUMAN?

We must now consider the key point in the entire discussion of abortion: Is the small embryo or fetus a human being, or merely a piece of tissue, without being, life, or rights? Those in favor of abortion take the latter position, stating that it does not look human and does not have full human characteristics, such as fully developed vision, human size and shape, the power of thought, or self-sufficiency. And, when it cannot yet live outside the uterus, it is not a "baby." Therefore, it is not human—and no harm is done by destroying it.

Misrepresentations and lack of understanding by educated people, regarding the fetus, are incomprehensible. At a state legislative hearing on abortion in Florida, some students and faculty members from the state university testified that, "The fetus is not human. It is a mass of protoplasm . . . a group of cells . . . a mass of tissue. It is a parasite which has no right to live." I have personally debated on radio and television state senators, physicians, and others advocating abortion, who have publicly stated that, "At 20 weeks pregnancy, you cannot tell the developing fetus from a cancer or a mass of flesh." (By contrast, see picture—The Human Fetus).

The opponents to aborticide point out that actually every characteristic the human will ever have is contained in the genes of the ovum and sperm, as soon as united. As an embryo, it is undergoing continual development. All it needs is time and

THE HUMAN FETUS—ACTUAL SIZE

8 weeks

9 weeks

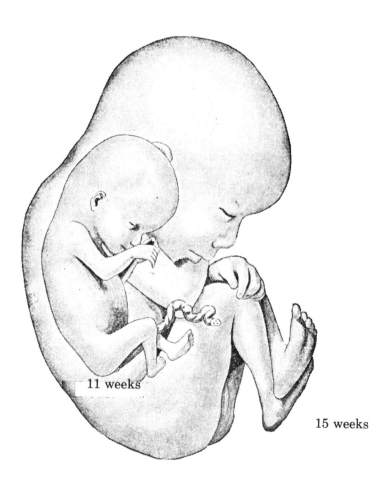

11 weeks

15 weeks

From *Developmental Anatomy—A Textbook of Embryology*
by
Leslie B. Arey, Ph. D., Sc. D., Ll. D.

nutrition, and only two avenues are open to it: It will be born a live human baby or be aborted as a dead human fetus. Either way, it is human—has anyone ever known a woman to reproduce any other species?

Development of the human embryo and fetus is rapid and amazing. In recent years, it has been very well documented through intrauterine photography, cardiography, electroencephalography, microscopy, and other techniques. Both brain and heart tracings are recordable and readable by eight weeks.

Arey's textbook of embryology, a world authority on human development, states that from 5 to 8 weeks gestation the head becomes erect, the face develops, the eyes, ears and nose appear, and the digits become demarcated. From 8 to 12 weeks, the fetus already has developed its human characteristics. Fingernails form, and sex can be distinguished externally. By 16 weeks, the face is distinctive in appearance, and individual differences become recognizable.

Dr. William Lynch, Boston gynecologist and obstetrician says, "You can't have it both ways. Medical scientists claim they are creating human life in a test tube. You can't call it something else in the womb." Dr. Richard V. Jaynes, of the American Board of Obstetrics and Gynecology, a Detroit physician and Presbyterian, "unalterably opposed to liberalized abortion laws," related the human nature of the fetus, when he described before a Michigan Senate Committee the procedure of abortion in which "after 10 to 12 weeks the baby has grown large enough that the head and larger parts must be crushed or cut into pieces and scooped out limb by limb."

While a fetus does not exactly resemble a young boy, neither does a baby exactly resemble an old man. Human life is one continuous cellular change, beginning with conception and ending with death. Legally and philsophically, throughout history, the fetus has been considered human. This position is made clear by quotations from court decisions in several states: "A child is not only regarded as a human being, but as such from the moment of conception—which it is in fact"—District of Columbia 1946. "Medical authorities have long recognized that a child is in existence from the moment of conception"—Illinois 1961. An unborn child is defined as "a human being from the time of its conception until it is born alive"—as defined by Wisconsin Abortion Statute, Criminal Code 904.04. "A fetus which has reached the age of viability is a human being for the

IS IT A PERSON OR A THING?

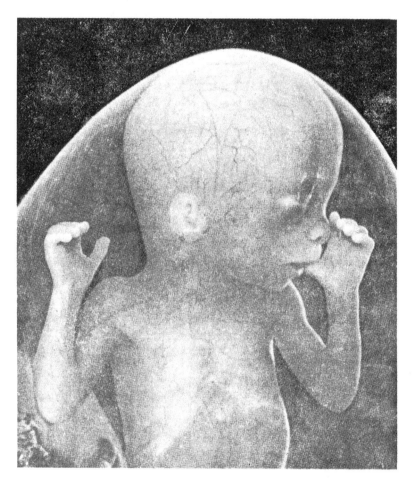

An 18-week-old fetus, now 6 inches long, sucking its thumb in the womb. (The gestation period of an average full-term pregnancy is 40 weeks.)

purposes of California homicide statutes"—California Appeals Court 1969. ". . . 'child' should include a human being upon conception and during pregnancy, as well as one actually born"—Colorado Supreme Court 1936, and restated in opinion of August 1969.

Rabbi Tibor Stern, of the Cohen Community Synagogue, Miami, states that, "Centuries of traditional Jewish law clearly establish the human nature of the unborn fetus and the immorality of abortion. Those Jews who support abortion legislation have erased every trace of Jewish law from their religion." States Professor Otto Piper, of Princeton Seminary (Protestant), "We have no right to destroy new life." And, Professor Karl Barth (Protestant), of Basel, "He who destroys germinating life kills a man." And, Dietrich Bonhoffer, Lutheran theologian killed by Hitler, "Abortion is nothing but murder." And, the Didache, one of the earliest known pieces of Christian writing, with its precept: "Thou shall not procure abortion."

Even *Life* magazine, whose editorial policy has supported abortion, stated, in "The Drama of Life Before Birth" (a magnificent picture story of the development of the human fetus), "The birth of a human life really occurs at the moment the mother's egg is fertilized by one of the father's sperm cells." Additionally, *Medical World News,* in a picture article of March 15, 1968, entitled "Close-up of Human Life Before Birth," shows an 11-week-old fetus, unmistakably human, with the picture caption: "All body systems in 2-1/2-inch-long fetus are now working."

Dr. Robert J. Luby, former Professor of Obstetrics and Gynecology at the University of Nebraska School of Medicine, and now Professor and Associate Director at Creighton Medical School, contends, "I am convinced that sometime after conception this being shares human destiny and has an equal right to life with all of us. The permissive legislation supporting abortion is a denial of this right."

Hundreds of other scientific, legal, and religious groups and papers could be quoted establishing the human nature of the fetus, condemning abortion, or opposing liberal abortion legislation, including: the Anglican Bishops of Australia; the Northern Indiana Convention of the Episcopal Church; the President of the Union of Orthodox Jewish Congregations of America; the President of the Rabbinical Council of America; the Catholic Bishops of America; world-famous heart surgeon, Dr. Christian Barnard;

Dr. J. Robert Nelson, Professor of Theology at Boston University; Dr. Albert C. Outler, Professor of Theology at Southern Methodist University; the famous evangelist, Dr. Billy Graham; and many more.

However, let us close with a quote from Rev. Arnim Polster, former attorney, and Lutheran pastor, Daly City, California: "The contention that human life begins at conception is heavily supported by the science of biology. Must not the law regard the fetus in the womb as a human being and grant it all the rights and protection that our laws extend to all human life? To deal with human life as if it were of no value cannot be right in the eyes of God or man. The gift of life is God-given. Can it be mercy to destroy life? Or shall "liberalized" abortion be given its rightful name—murder?"

WHERE WILL IT LEAD?

One must recognize that the permissive appetite is never satisfied, and that any liberalization of the abortion law is but the first step for many of those most vigorously proposing abortion. It begins with "updating archaic abortion laws" or "abortion reform," followed by *liberal abortion, abortion on demand at any stage, infanticide* and, finally, *euthanasia*.

The "program is no longer speculative. The cruel, inhuman, atheistic "new world order" is becoming a reality—a scientific, computerized society, in which every aspect of our lives is controlled—even our birth, life and death. One Nobel Prize winning scientist has suggested that newborn babies be given tests and a period of evaluation. Those who meet the standards would then be given birth certificates—the others destroyed, and considered not legally born. The Chief of Pediatrics at one of our universities wrote that he favored legal abortion and added that he also recommended infanticide, ". . . where well born or minorly defective children can be exterminated before the 12th month of post-gestational life [after birth] without causing concern to the society as a whole."

There are many other experts in medicine, sociology, population control, and government who would lead us into a new world of controlled life and death. The threat is everywhere evident today, but nowhere has the plan been more clearly stated than in an editorial in the official journal of the California Medical Association, September, 1970. I quote at length:

26

"The traditional Western ethic has always placed great emphasis on the intrinsic worth and equal value of every human life. This ethic has had the blessing of the Judeo-Christian heritage and has been the basis for most of our laws and much of our social policy and has also been a keystone of Western medicine . . . This traditional ethic is still clearly dominant, but there is much to suggest that it is being eroded at its core and may eventually even be abandoned . . . Since the old ethic has not yet been fully displaced it has been necessary to separate the idea of abortion from the idea of killing, which continues to be socially abhorrent. The result has been a curious avoidance of the scientific fact, which everyone really knows, that human life begins at conception and is continuous whether intra or extra-uterine until death. The very considerable semantic gymnastics which are required to rationalize abortion as anything but taking a human life would be ludicrous if they were not often put forth under socially impeccable auspices. It is suggested that this schizophrenic sort of subterfuge is necessary because while a new ethic is being accepted the old one has not yet been rejected.

"Medicine's role with respect to changing attitudes toward abortion may well be a prototype of what is to occur . . . One may anticipate further development of these roles as the problems of birth control and birth selection are extended inevitably to death selection and death control whether by the individual or by society . . . It is not too early for our profession to examine the new ethic, and prepare to apply it in a rational development for the fulfillment and betterment of mankind in what is almost certain to be a biologically oriented world society."

However, men of greater wisdom, in all professions and from all nations, have warned us, men such as Dr. R. A. Gallop, Professor and Chairman, Department of Food Science, University of Manitoba (Canada), and an international authority on pollution, food supply and demography. According to him, the logic is irrefutable—once you allow the killing of unborn babies, there will be no stopping, there will be no age limit, there will be no safety for any living human. Eventually, you will be the victim. Even your children will kill you—because you permitted the killing of their brothers and sisters, or because of your money and estates. If the courts allow it for some, they will allow it for you. If a doctor will kill a baby in the womb for a fee, he will kill you with a needle when your children or the government pays. This is your horrible nightmare.

CONCLUSION

Certainly, many legislators and physicians who have advocated liberal abortion have had good intentions, and I have given consideration both to their sincere motives and to the arguments with which they support their position. However, thorough and logical analysis must lead to these conclusions:

1. Life—some type of growing, metabolic organism, which has all the potentials necessary for developing, *fully and only,* into a human being—begins at conception.

2. Legally, philosophically, and scientifically this life has always been regarded as human. Modern medical science now clearly demonstrates the human nature of this life.

3. Aborticide has been condemned throughout history by Law, Medicine, and Judeo-Christian teaching.

4. There is no medical necessity, physical or mental, for aborticide. Convenience, yes; real necessity, no.

5. The right of the unborn child to life must outweigh the desires of others to destroy it, whatever the basis of these desires.

6. The liberalization of abortion laws now will ultimately lead to legalized extermination of other humans, and will be another step in the decaying moral values of our current society.

Moreover, I concur with the late Dr. Edward Lauth that society can solve the problem of the illegal abortionist by better law enforcement. Society and the physician can solve the problem of the rapist and incestuous man by better mental health facilities and earlier treatment. Physicians are very able to assist the ill and disturbed mother through her pregnancy and, with good judgment and the help of research, prevent deformities in her baby.

Physicians are in the high profession of healing, not in the low business of abortion. That great physician and humanitarian, Dr. Albert Schweitzer, said it clearly: "Reverence for life, life of all kinds, is the first principle of civilization." No physician, no parent, no hospital group, no legislative assmbly or government has the right to take innocent life. As one senator stated when members of the Florida Senate were debating as to whether the decision to "terminate a pregnancy" should be left up to doctors or to lawyers, "I offer a third alternative—that it be left up to God, and the child be permitted to live."

WHAT CAN WE DO?

1. Thoroughly understand the information and arguments presented in *Abortion: Yes or No,* so that you can present that particular issue well when the occasion arises.
2. Distribute this booklet to churches, civic clubs, high schools, nursing and medical schools, libraries, religion classes, and right-to-life organizations.
3. Give a copy of this booklet to questioning young people and to those who are neutral on the issue or even in favor of abortion —especially women.
4. Also give this booklet to married couples and to those contemplating marriage.
5. In particular, give a copy of this booklet to women who might procure an abortion.
6. Write short, clear and effective Letters to the Editor of your area newspapers and any other publications in which you have an opportunity to express your views. Call in to radio talk shows whenever possible.
7. Permission is granted to quote from *Abortion: Yes or No,* provided it is used or printed exactly as written, and proper identification and authorship are given. The information in this booklet can be used whenever and however it will help you in your fight against abortion.
8. We urge you to write your Governor and State Legislators, asking them to defeat or repeal all pro-abortion legislation and all bills advocating mercy killing in any form. Request that they also pass a bill or a resolution calling for a pro-life constitutional amendment. Urge your U.S. Senators and Representatives to support a constitutional amendment to protect the right to life of all citizens, from the moment of conception until natural death. There can be no compromise with evil, even if the courts judge it to be good.
9. Join our effort to defend the rights and dignity of human life, and to help preserve this great nation and our civilization. Send your orders for *Abortion: Yes or No* to:

Telephone your order, using VISA, MasterCard or Discover. Tel. 1-815-226-7777. TOLL FREE: 1-800-437-5876.

10. Dr. Grady will be happy to provide you with a wide range of material and publications important to you and your family. Much of this information is not readily available through the public media. You may write to him at:

Americans For The Right To Life
John L. Grady, M.D., Chairman
Benton, Tennessee 37307

Americans For The Right To Life is a non-profit, volunteer organization, which pays no salaries and has no fixed overhead. All contributions go to the publication and distribution of this booklet and similar material. Every donation is greatly appreciated and carefully used. Contributors of $5 or more will receive a permanent life membership in Americans For The Right To Life and receive a beautiful certificate to that effect.

QUANTITY DISCOUNT
Priced low for mass distribution

1	copy	3.00
5	copies	1.50 each
10	copies	1.25 each
25	copies	1.00 each
50	copies	.90 each
100	copies	.80 each
500	copies	.70 each
1,000	copies	.60 each

U.S. & CAN. POST/HDLG: On orders of $1-$10, add $2.00; $10.01-$20, add $3.00; $20.01-$30, add $4.00; $30.01-$50, add $5.00; $50.01-$75, add $6.00; $75.01-up, add $7.00.

Check, Visa, MasterCard, or Discover accepted.

TAN BOOKS AND PUBLISHERS, INC.
P.O. Box 424, Rockford, Illinois 61105
Call Toll Free: 1-800-437-5876

WILL IT BE THIS?

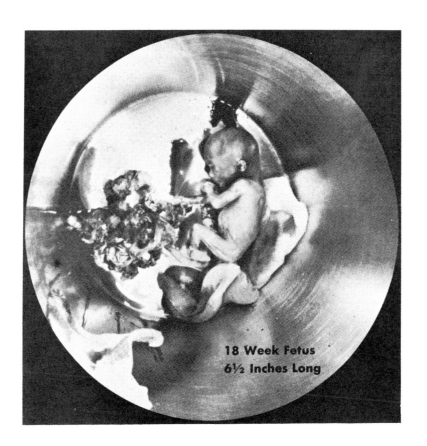

18 Week Fetus
6½ Inches Long

OR, WILL IT BE THIS?